-19
2
4-16

SCIENCE DISCOVERY

Space

Q&A

Edward Willett

MEDIA ENHANCED BOOKS

AV2 BY WEIGL

ADDED VALUE • AUDIO VISUAL

www.av2books.com

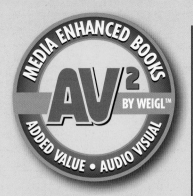

AV² provides enriched content that supplements and complements this book. Weigl's AV² books strive to create inspired learning and engage young minds in a total learning experience.

Your AV² Media Enhanced books come alive with...

Audio
Listen to sections of the book read aloud.

Key Words
Study vocabulary, and complete a matching word activity.

Video
Watch informative video clips.

Quizzes
Test your knowledge.

Embedded Weblinks
Gain additional information for research.

Slide Show
View images and captions, and prepare a presentation.

Try This!
Complete activities and hands-on experiments.

... and much, much more!

Go to **www.av2books.com**, and enter this book's unique code.

BOOK CODE

T 4 4 4 0

AV² by Weigl brings you media enhanced books that support active learning.

Published by AV² by Weigl
350 5th Avenue, 59th Floor
New York, NY 10118
Websites: www.av2books.com   www.weigl.com

Library of Congress Control Number: 2013953156
ISBN 978-1-4896-0692-1 (hardcover)
ISBN 978-1-4896-0693-8 (softcover)
ISBN 978-1-4896-0694-5 (single-user eBook)
ISBN 978-1-4896-0695-2 (multi-user eBook)

Printed in the United States of America, in North Mankato, Minnesota
1 2 3 4 5 6 7 8 9 0 18 17 16 15 14

042014
WEP301113

Project Coordinator Aaron Carr
Designer Mandy Christiansen

Every reasonable effort has been made to trace ownership and to obtain permission to reprint copyright material. The publishers would be pleased to have any errors or omissions brought to their attention so that they may be corrected in subsequent printings.

Photo Credits
Weigl acknowledges Getty Images as its primary photo supplier for this title.

Contents

What Is Space?

Outer space, often simply called space, is the part of the **universe** beyond Earth's **atmosphere**. Many scientists think the universe started with a huge explosion called the Big Bang. They believe this occurred between 11 billion and 20 billion years ago.

In recent years, human journeys into space have given scientists a great deal of information about it. Spacecraft without human crews have traveled to the edge of, and even beyond, Earth's solar system. This solar system includes the Sun, as well as the **planets** and other objects that orbit, or travel around, the Sun. The Hubble Space Telescope, which orbits Earth, has allowed scientists to see deeper into outer space than ever before.

How Scientists Use Inquiry to Answer Questions

When scientists try to answer a question, they follow the process of scientific inquiry. They begin by making observations and asking questions. Then, they propose an answer to their question. This is called the hypothesis. The hypothesis guides scientists as they research the issue. Research can involve performing experiments or reading books on the subject. When their research is finished, scientists examine their results and review their hypothesis. Often, they discover that their hypothesis was incorrect. If this happens, they revise their hypothesis and go through the process of scientific inquiry again.

Process of Scientific Inquiry

Observation

The universe includes many large empty regions. Within space, there are also objects of different types and sizes. What exactly is in space?

Have You Answered the Question?

The cycle of scientific inquiry never truly ends. More research and experiments may be needed to test new hypotheses. Once scientists know that there are many exoplanets, they may ask, "Could life exist on some of these planets?"

Research

Scientists studying space try to learn about objects beyond Earth's solar system. They ask questions such as, "What is in space similar to or different from what we know?"

Results

Scientists have recently discovered a number of exoplanets. Some seem to be very similar to planets in Earth's solar system.

Hypothesis

Scientists have located exoplanets, which are planets not in Earth's solar system. They have hypothesized that there are other exoplanets that cannot be seen.

Experiment

To test this hypothesis, scientists measure the brightness of stars. When a planet crosses the face of its star, it blocks some of the star's light. A specially designed telescope records the change in brightness.

What Types of Objects Are in Space?

The largest bodies in space are stars and planets. Many of the planets in Earth's solar system have moons. It may be that exoplanets have moons, too. Dwarf planets have some features of both planets and moons. In Earth's solar system, asteroids, meteoroids, and comets orbit the Sun.

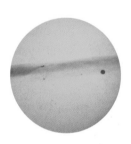

Star

A star is a huge, hot, glowing ball of gas. The heat is produced when hydrogen gas deep inside the star changes to helium. This change also releases energy in the form of heat. Earth's Sun is a medium-sized star compared to others in space.

Planet

A planet is a large sphere. Often, it orbits a star in a path that has an **oval** shape. Planets reflect light from the star they orbit, but they do not shine on their own.

Dwarf Planet

Dwarf planets in Earth's solar system are spheres that look like small planets. They orbit the Sun, but unlike a planet, they have other objects besides moons within their orbits.

Moon

A moon is a natural **satellite** of a planet. The number of moons that different planets have varies. Some planets have a large number of moons, and some have a few or none. Earth has one.

Asteroid

Asteroids are rocky objects that orbit the Sun. Asteroids are smaller than planets and dwarf planets, but they are larger than meteoroids.

Meteoroid

A meteoroid is a small piece of stone or metal. A meteoroid that enters Earth's atmosphere and burns is called a meteor. Sometimes, part of a meteor reaches the ground. This piece is called a meteorite.

Comet

A comet is a ball of dust and frozen gas with a long tail. Its tail can be as long as 155 million miles (250 million kilometers). Comets travel in long oval-shaped orbits that bring them close to Sun at certain times and take them very far from it at other times.

Cosmic Dust

Tiny **particles** of solid material float around in space between stars. Called cosmic dust, these particles can look like smoke. If enough cosmic dust comes together, this material can help form new stars and planets.

Digging Deeper

Your Challenge!

Scientists have been using the Hubble Space Telescope to learn about objects in space. The new James Webb Space Telescope (JWST) is planned to go into operation in 2018. To dig deeper into the issue:

Using the website of the National Aeronautics and Space Administration (NASA) and other sources, research the JWST. In what ways is it similar to Hubble? What are several ways in which it is different? What are some things that scientists hope to learn from the JWST?

Summary

In addition to stars and planets, space contains other types of bodies, as well as cosmic dust.

Further Inquiry

As scientists learn more about objects in space, maybe we should ask:

What is in Earth's solar system?

What Is in Earth's Solar System?

The solar system is made up of the Sun and everything that orbits it. This includes eight planets and five dwarf planets. The Sun keeps all other objects in orbit because of its powerful **gravity**. This force keeps objects from flying off into space.

Each planet has its own orbit. Mercury is closest to the Sun, followed by Venus, Earth, and Mars. These four planets, called the inner planets, are made of rock.

Earth's Solar System

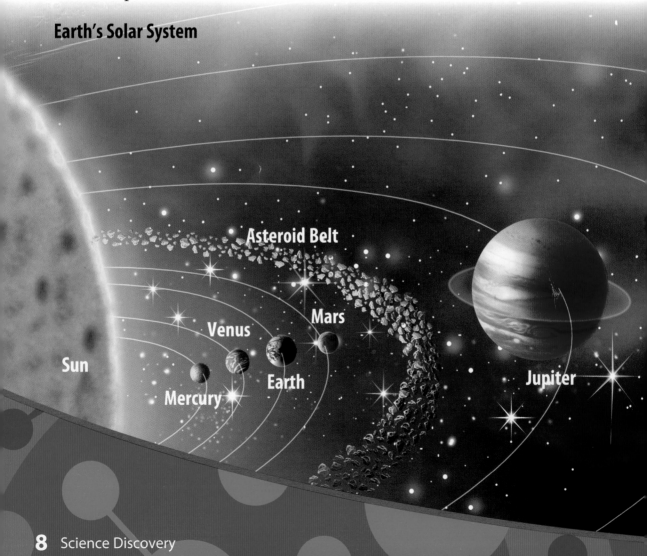

Sun

Mercury

Venus

Earth

Mars

Asteroid Belt

Jupiter

Jupiter, Saturn, Uranus, and Neptune are the four outer planets. They are the largest planets in the solar system and are made mostly of gas. They are known as the gas giants.

All planets except Mercury and Venus have one or more moons. Two dwarf planets, Pluto and Eris, also have moons. Each planet and dwarf planet has its own gravity. These forces keep the solar system's moons in orbit.

Digging Deeper

Your Challenge!

The Sun's gravity is pulling everything in the solar system toward it. To dig deeper into the issue:

Research why planets and other bodies stay in orbit, instead of crashing into the Sun. What other forces are affecting the path these bodies take as they travel through space?

Summary

The solar system includes eight planets and many other objects that orbit the Sun.

Further Inquiry

Since the Sun is the center of the solar system, maybe we should ask:

What is the Sun like?

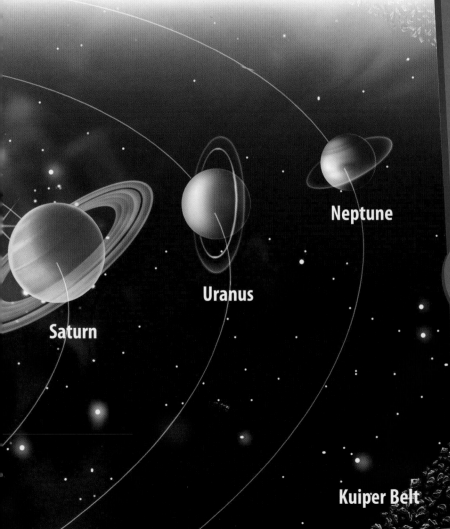

Neptune

Uranus

Saturn

Kuiper Belt

Q&A

What Is the Sun Like?

The Sun is the largest body in the solar system. It is more than 100 times the size of Earth. The Sun does not look very large in the sky because it is far from Earth. It is about 92.6 million miles (149.6 million km) away.

At the Sun's surface, the temperature is about 10,000° Fahrenheit (5,540° Celsius). Inside the Sun, temperatures are much higher. They can reach 27 million degrees Fahrenheit (15 million degrees Celsius). Heat and light from the Sun reach all other objects in the solar system. Without the Sun's heat, Earth would be a frozen rock on which no plants, animals, or people could live.

❭ The surface of the Sun is almost 100 times warmer than the hottest day in the hottest desert on Earth.

The Sun looks different from other stars in the sky because the other stars are much farther from Earth. Many stars in the universe are larger, brighter, and hotter than the Sun. However, because they are billions of miles (km) from Earth, they appear as dots of light and often can be seen only at night.

⌃ Plants on Earth use energy from the Sun to make their own food. This process is called photosynthesis.

Your Challenge!

From Earth, other stars look much smaller than the Sun because they are much farther away. To dig deeper into the issue:

Using books or websites, research which star, other than the Sun, is closest to Earth. How far from Earth is this star? What does it look like in the night sky?

Summary

The Sun is a huge ball of very hot gases that sends heat and light into the solar system. Life on Earth depends upon the heat the planet receives from the Sun.

Further Inquiry

The Sun affects the solar system in other ways besides giving off heat and light. Maybe we should ask:

What are sunspots, solar flares, and solar wind?

What Are Sunspots, Solar Flares, and Solar Wind?

Sunspots are dark areas that appear at times on the Sun. For centuries, no one understood what caused sunspots. Scientists now know that these spots appear black because they are much cooler than the rest of the Sun's surface. Sunspots seem to move across the surface of the Sun, but they do not really. The entire Sun rotates, or spins. This causes sunspots to appear to be moving when seen from Earth.

Sunspot activity tends to follow an 11-year cycle, going from a period with few sunspots or none to a period with many sunspots. The sunspot cycle may affect Earth's climate. For example, when the number of sunspots is highest, the southeastern United States seems to have colder than normal temperatures.

❭ Eruptions of hot gas from the Sun can be thousands of miles (km) long.

▲ The colors of the northern and southern lights depend on the type of gas particles in the atmosphere affected by the solar wind.

Solar flares are brief, huge explosions on the Sun's surface. They often occur near sunspots, and they send large amounts of **radiation** into space. When some of this radiation reaches Earth, it can interfere with radio broadcasts and even cause power blackouts. Sometimes, giant loops of extremely hot gas erupt from the Sun and stretch into space.

At all times, the Sun sends out more than 1 million tons (907,000 tonnes) of gas particles per second. This stream of particles is called the solar wind. Particles take about three days to travel from the Sun to Earth. The solar wind causes the colorful displays in the sky called the northern lights and southern lights. Most often seen at night, the light displays tend to occur over areas near the North and South Poles.

Digging Deeper

Your Challenge!

A Sun-related event caused serious problems in Quebec, Canada, on March 13, 1989. To dig deeper into the issue:

Research what happened on that day. What solar event had occurred shortly before? What were the effects of this event in Quebec and other areas on Earth?

Summary

Sunspots and solar flares are changes on the Sun's surface that may affect climate and radio signals on Earth. The solar wind is a stream of gas particles that goes out from the Sun into the solar system.

Further Inquiry

The Sun has major effects on other planets, as well as Earth. Maybe we should ask:

What is Mercury like?

What Is Mercury Like?

The planet closest to the Sun, Mercury receives more of the Sun's heat than any other body in the solar system. Mercury's highest temperature is more than 800°F (425°C). This is hot enough to melt some types of metal.

However, the planet can also be very cold. Mercury rotates on its **axis**. As it spins, each area on the planet sometimes faces the Sun and is sometimes in darkness. Like Earth, Mercury has daylight and night. Unlike Earth, however, Mercury has no atmosphere. A planet's atmosphere can act like a blanket to hold in heat. Without an atmosphere, the parts of Mercury in darkness lose heat very quickly at night. The coldest temperatures on Mercury are about −280°F (−175°C). That is more than twice as cold as the lowest temperature ever recorded on Earth.

Mercury is the smallest planet in the solar system. It is about one-third Earth's size. One orbit of the Sun is a planet's year. Mercury's trip around the Sun, or year, is less than one-fourth of a year on Earth. However, Mercury is very slow to spin completely around on its axis. One complete spin is a planet's day. Mercury's day is as long as 58 days on Earth.

No human has ever visited Mercury. Two spacecraft, *Mariner 10* and *Messenger*, have explored Mercury from just above its surface. Scientists know that it looks like Earth's Moon. Mercury has **craters**, deposits of lava that flowed out of volcanoes, and dust-covered hills and plains. One crater is larger than the state of Texas.

❯ After more than 2,000 orbits of Mercury, the *Messenger* spacecraft completed taking pictures of the planet's entire surface.

Digging Deeper

Your Challenge!

The *Messenger* spacecraft started to orbit Mercury and send back information in 2011. To dig deeper into the issue:

Research the types of information scientists have received from *Messenger*. Make a list of three to five facts about Mercury that were not known before *Messenger* reached the planet.

Summary

Mercury, the planet closest to the Sun, is the smallest planet in the solar system. It is extremely hot in the day and cold at night.

Further Inquiry

In many ways, Mercury is very different from Earth. Other planets may be more similar. Maybe we should ask:

What is Venus like?

What Is Venus Like?

Venus is the planet closest to Earth. It is about the same size as Earth and has an atmosphere. For many years, it was difficult for scientists to study the surface of Venus because the planet is constantly covered with clouds. Science fiction writers used to imagine that, beneath its clouds, Venus had huge oceans and jungles. Today, people know this is not true.

In the 20th century, scientists began using **radar** to learn about the surface of Venus. They found that it has many types of land formations found on Earth. These include canyons, valleys, mountains, craters, and plains. The first spacecraft to visit Venus was the *Venera 3* **probe**, which landed on the planet in 1966. This and later probes have provided a great deal of information about Venus.

⌄ Scientists know of at least 1,600 volcanoes on Venus, more than any other planet in the solar system.

Venus's atmosphere is mostly carbon dioxide and has no oxygen. On Earth, more than 20 percent of the atmosphere is oxygen and much less than 1 percent is carbon dioxide. Humans could not breathe on Venus. Carbon dioxide traps a great deal of the heat from the Sun. Temperatures on Venus can reach almost 900°F (480°C).

The planet's clouds are made of sulfuric acid, which can quickly burn human skin. The clouds covering Venus reflect sunlight very well. This is why Venus is easy to see from Earth in the night sky.

⌃ Venus is the brightest object in the night sky except for the Moon.

Your Challenge!

Venus is similar to Earth in some ways. In other ways, it is very different. To dig deeper into the issue:

Research Venus's orbit and rotation on its axis. How long does it take the planet to go around the Sun once? How long is one day on Venus? If a person could stand on Venus, why would the Sun appear to rise in the west and set in the east?

Summary

Venus has an atmosphere that is almost all carbon dioxide and is covered by thick clouds of sulfuric acid. Humans could not survive there.

Further Inquiry

The planet closest to Venus is Earth. Maybe we should ask:

What is Earth like?

What Is Earth Like?

When seen from space, Earth is a mixture of green, brown, and blue beneath swirling white clouds. The green and brown areas are the continents and large islands. The blue areas are oceans, which cover nearly 70 percent of the planet's surface. In addition to the oceans, Earth has liquid water in lakes, rivers, and streams. It also has frozen water in **glaciers** and in areas around the North and South Poles.

Scientists have discovered ice and water on other planets and moons in the solar system. However, as far as they know, Earth is the only planet or moon that has liquid water on its surface all the time. All forms of life on Earth need water to survive.

Earth's atmosphere is made up mostly of nitrogen and oxygen. The atmosphere protects people and other living things from harmful radiation from the Sun. It also keeps temperatures from getting too cold for living things to survive.

Earth rotates on its axis at about 1,000 miles (1,600 km) per hour. At this speed, Earth makes one spin in 24 hours. At the same time, Earth is traveling around the Sun at more than 66,000 miles (107,000 km) per hour. Its orbit around the Sun is 584 million miles (940 million km) long. A complete trip around the Sun takes 365.25 days.

> Earth's rocky crust, the planet's outer layer, is about 6 to 40 miles (10 to 65 km) thick.

▼ Huge glaciers near the coast of Alaska move toward the Gulf of Alaska and the Pacific Ocean.

Digging Deeper

Your Challenge!

Like other planets, Earth has many noteworthy features. To dig deeper into the issue:

Make a list of extreme features of Earth, such as the highest point, lowest point, hottest place, coldest place, wettest place, driest place, and windiest place. Research the locations of these places and plot them on a map of the world.

Summary

Earth is the only planet known to have liquid water all the time. Its atmosphere helps make conditions on the planet right for the survival of living things.

Further Inquiry

If Earth has everything it needs to support life, perhaps its neighbor planet does, too. Maybe we should ask:

What is Mars like?

What Is Mars Like?

In the 19th century, **astronomers** studying Mars using telescopes thought they saw straight lines that were canals on the surface of the planet. For many years, some people thought there is life on Mars. Spacecraft that have visited Mars in recent years have shown that there are no canals and no life on the planet. There is some evidence, however, that Mars could have supported **microorganisms** in the past.

The surface of Mars is a rocky, dusty desert. Strong winds blow the dust across the planet's surface. Sometimes, the entire planet is covered with one huge dust storm. Mars has the tallest known volcano and the deepest known canyon in the solar system. Olympus Mons is 16 miles (25 km) tall. Valles Marineris is almost 4 miles (6.5 km) deep.

Like Venus, Mars has a carbon dioxide atmosphere. However, Mars's atmosphere is very thin. This means there is not a great deal of gas in each cubic inch (cubic centimeter) of space. As a result, the atmosphere does not hold in heat well. Although temperatures on some parts of Mars can reach 80°F (27°C), the planet is mostly very cold. Its average temperature is about –40°F (–4°C).

Mars is a little more than half as big as Earth. Its day is almost exactly the same length, 24 hours and 37 minutes. Mars has two small moons, named Phobos and Deimos.

❯ NASA has landed rovers, which are robotic vehicles controlled from Earth, on the surface of Mars.

Future plans for exploring the rugged, rocky surface of Mars include using balloons and glider planes dropped from spacecraft.

Digging Deeper

Your Challenge!

More spacecraft have been sent to Mars than any other body in the solar system except Earth's Moon. To dig deeper into the issue:

Research one of the rovers that have landed on Mars, such as *Curiosity* or *Opportunity*. Using words and pictures, make a chart or poster showing NASA's goals for the rover, some of the vehicle's major discoveries, and any failures the rover has had.

Summary

Mars is a rocky, dusty planet. It may have had life in the past, but there are no signs of life today.

Further Inquiry

Beyond Mars, there are many chunks of rock orbiting the Sun. Maybe we should ask:

What is the asteroid belt?

What Is the Asteroid Belt?

Between Mars and Jupiter, there is an area in which millions of rocky or metallic objects orbit the Sun. This region is called the asteroid belt. The largest object in the asteroid belt is the dwarf planet Ceres, which is about 620 miles (1,000 km) across. This area of the solar system may also contain hundreds of thousands of asteroids at least 0.6 miles (1 km) wide. Most asteroids in the solar system are found between Mars and Jupiter, but some exist in other regions.

Sometimes, two asteroids crash into each other, and pieces break off. The smaller pieces are meteoroids. They may be as small as a grain of sand. However, some meteoroids are 3 feet (1 meter) wide or more.

❯ A meteoroid entering Earth's atmosphere may be traveling as fast as 12 miles (20 km) per second.

A meteoroid that enters Earth's atmosphere becomes very hot. This occurs because of **friction** between the fast-moving meteoroid and the air. As the meteoroid slows down, some of its energy of motion is changed to heat energy. The heat causes most meteors to burn up in the atmosphere. Sometimes, when a meteoroid enters the atmosphere at night, a bright streak of light can be seen across the sky.

Many meteorites that survive the trip through the atmosphere and reach Earth's surface are very small. Small meteorites have dented cars and smashed holes in the roofs of houses. Large meteorites can cause more severe damage if they do not land in remote areas.

⌃ A meteorite striking Earth's surface leaves a crater 10 to 20 times larger than the object itself.

Digging Deeper

Your Challenge!

It is unlikely but possible that a large asteroid could hit Earth. To dig deeper into the issue:

Some scientists believe that most types of dinosaurs died out 65 million years ago because an asteroid struck Earth. Research this theory. What is the evidence for an asteroid strike? What results of the impact could make dinosaurs and other living things unable to survive?

Summary

The asteroid belt is the region of the solar system between Mars and Jupiter that contains thousands of asteroids and meteoroids orbiting the Sun.

Further Inquiry

A huge planet orbits the Sun on the far side of the asteroid belt. Maybe we should ask:

What is Jupiter like?

What Is Jupiter Like?

Jupiter is the largest planet in the solar system. It is more than 11 times as wide as Earth. Jupiter is made up mainly of hydrogen and helium and has no solid surface. Beneath theses gases, Jupiter is a huge ball of liquid. Jupiter puts out more heat than it receives from the Sun. Scientists do not know why this occurs.

Great Red Spot

⌃ Jupiter's Great Red Spot is more than twice the size of Earth.

▲ Jupiter's moon Io has more than 400 volcanoes.

Four rings made of dust and small pieces of rock circle the planet. The rocky particles are so small that the rings cannot be seen from Earth. They were discovered when the *Voyager 2* probe flew past Jupiter in 1979. Jupiter also has the biggest and longest-lasting storm in the solar system. Called the Great Red Spot, this hurricane-like storm has lasted for at least 400 years.

Jupiter has more moons than any other planet. Using information from probes and space telescopes, astronomers have found more than 60 moons. They continue to search for other moons of Jupiter and the planets beyond it. Jupiter's largest moon, Ganymede, is the biggest moon in the solar system. In fact, it is larger than the planet Mercury. Another moon, Europa, is completely covered with a frozen ocean.

Digging Deeper

Your Challenge!

All of the four outer planets have a large number of moons. To dig deeper into the issue:

Research the moons of Jupiter, Saturn, Uranus, and Neptune. Make a chart showing the number of moons known to orbit each planet, the largest moon of each, and several facts about that moon.

Summary

Jupiter, the largest planet, also has the biggest moon and storm in the solar system.

Further Inquiry

Jupiter's rings were discovered only recently. The next planet beyond Jupiter is well-known for its rings. Maybe we should ask:

What is Saturn like?

What Is Saturn Like?

For centuries, scientists have been studying Saturn's colorful rings. The Italian astronomer Galileo Galilei saw them using a telescope in the 1600s. The rings are made of particles ranging from tiny specks of dust to icy chunks many feet (m) wide.

Scientists do not know for sure how the rings formed, but they have several theories. One is that Saturn's very strong gravity caused comets, asteroids, or moons to break up while orbiting the planet. The pieces kept crashing into each other and breaking into smaller and smaller chunks. Over time, the smallest pieces spread out around Saturn to form its rings.

Like Jupiter, Saturn is made of gas and liquid. Its atmosphere is a thick layer of gases. Also like Jupiter, it gives off more heat than it receives.

Saturn is slightly smaller than Jupiter, but it is still almost 10 times the size of Earth. A day on Saturn is short. It takes only 10.5 hours for the planet to rotate once on its axis. The length of Saturn's orbit is almost 5.6 billion miles (9 billion km). A year on Saturn is 30 times as long as a year on Earth.

❯ When Galileo first saw Saturn's rings through a telescope, he thought he was looking at three planets.

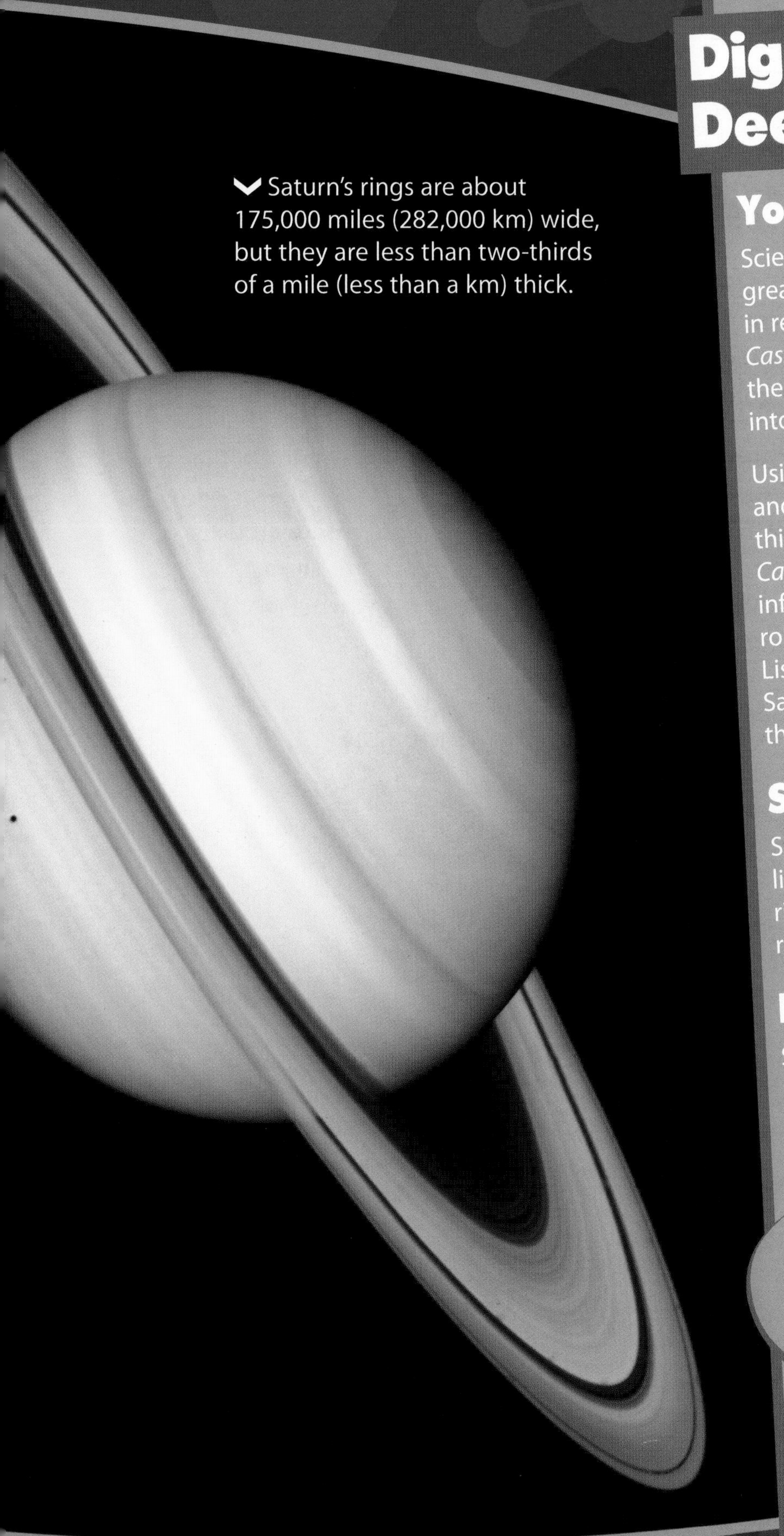

▼ Saturn's rings are about 175,000 miles (282,000 km) wide, but they are less than two-thirds of a mile (less than a km) thick.

Digging Deeper

Your Challenge!

Scientists have learned a great deal about Saturn in recent years from the *Cassini-Huygens* mission to the planet. To dig deeper into the issue:

Using the NASA website and other sources, research this mission. How has the *Cassini* spacecraft gathered information? What is the role of the *Huygens* probe? List several facts about Saturn learned from the mission.

Summary

Saturn, made of gas and liquid, is known for its rings. It rotates very rapidly on its axis.

Further Inquiry

Saturn and Jupiter are not the only planets in the solar system with rings. Maybe we should ask:

What is Uranus like?

What Is Uranus Like?

Uranus is made of icy gases and liquid. Its atmosphere is a layer of swirling gases and clouds. Winds reach speeds of 560 miles (900 km) per hour. The atmosphere contains methane gas, which gives the planet a bright blue color.

Much smaller than Jupiter or Saturn, Uranus is still more than four times the size of Earth. Like Jupiter and Saturn, Uranus has rings. In fact, it has at least 13 of them. The first rings were discovered by scientists viewing the planet with powerful telescopes in the 1970s. *Voyager 2* gathered more information about the rings when it flew by Uranus in the 1980s.

> Uranus's moon Miranda has large regions covered with ridges and valleys.

The planet is very cold, with temperatures lower than −350°F (−210°C). However, *Voyager 2* discovered an ocean of boiling water on Uranus's surface. The way Uranus spins on its axis is unique. Compared to all the other planets, Uranus rotates on its side rather than in an upright position like a top.

Digging Deeper

Your Challenge!

Some scientists have a theory that the way Uranus spins is the result of a collision. To dig deeper into the issue:

Research what scientists think may have happened to Uranus. Then, imagine that you were watching through a powerful telescope when this event took place. Write a news article describing and commenting on what you observed.

Summary

Known as the blue planet, Uranus is made of frozen gases and liquid. It has strong winds and more than a dozen rings.

Further Inquiry

The stormiest planet in the solar system is the one most distant from the Sun. Maybe we should ask:

What is Neptune like?

What Is Neptune Like?

Slightly smaller than Uranus, Neptune is the planet in the solar system farthest from the Sun. It is about 2.8 billion miles (4.5 billion km) away. It takes Neptune about 165 Earth years to orbit the Sun once.

Huge storms on Neptune are about ten times as strong as the most powerful hurricanes on Earth. The wind in Neptune's storms can blow at 1,500 miles (2,400 km) per hour. In 1989, when it flew past Neptune, *Voyager 2* sent back information about a giant hurricane-like storm. Called the Great Dark Spot, the storm was as big as Earth. A few years later, the Great Dark Spot was gone. However, in recent years, scientists have seen new dark spots in images of Neptune sent from the Hubble Space Telescope.

Neptune is a huge ball of icy gases and liquid. Like Uranus, it is blue because of methane gas in its atmosphere. Scientists think that Neptune may have a solid core of rock and ice about the size of Earth. Even though it is farther from the Sun than Uranus, Neptune is warmer. Like Jupiter and Saturn, Neptune puts out more heat than it receives from the Sun. Neptune has six known rings and at least 13 moons. Its largest moon, Triton, has a solid crust of ice.

Great Dark Spot

⌃ Before it disappeared, the storm called the Great Dark Spot moved across the surface of Neptune at a speed of almost 750 miles (1,200 km) an hour.

Digging Deeper

Your Challenge!

The planets of the solar system vary in size. To dig deeper into the issue:

Create a model of the solar system. You can use a marble for Mercury, a walnut for Venus, a golf ball for Earth, an acorn for Mars, a basketball for Jupiter, a soccer ball for Saturn, a softball for Uranus, and a grapefruit for Neptune. In this model a raisin can represent Earth's Moon. The Sun would have to be ball about 8 feet (2.5 m) high and wide.

Summary

Scientists studying Neptune have found at least 13 moons.

Further Inquiry

After *Voyager 2* passed Neptune, it continued past the far end of the solar system. Maybe we should ask:

What are the Kuiper belt and the Oort cloud?

⌃ Geysers on Neptune's moon Triton send cold liquid into the sky. The liquid freezes and falls back on Triton as snow.

What Are the Kuiper Belt and the Oort Cloud?

Billions of miles (km) from the Sun, beyond the orbit of Neptune, lies the Kuiper belt. Scientists believe it contains more than 70,000 objects that are orbiting the Sun. Astronomers continue to find and identify new objects.

One of the largest bodies in the Kuiper belt is Pluto. This dwarf planet is about 1,430 miles (2,300 km) across, a little more than one-sixth the size of Earth. Pluto has five moons, the largest number for any dwarf planet. Other dwarf planets in the Kuiper belt are Haumea, Makemake, and Eris. The most distant dwarf planet from the Sun, Eris may be larger than Pluto. Scientists hope that space probes will return more information about Eris.

Even farther from the Sun is the Oort cloud. This is a swarm of icy objects at the outer edge of the solar system. It may contain as many as 2 trillion bodies orbiting the Sun.

Short-term comets have orbits that take them as far from the Sun as the Kuiper belt. Long-term comets have orbits that extend to the Oort cloud. When it is farthest from the Sun, a comet may be a ball of ice only a few miles (km) across. As it gets closer to the Sun, the ice turns to gases. The ball, called the comet's head, may become thousands of miles (km) wide. The solar wind blows gases away from the head to form the comet's long tail. Short-term comets may complete one orbit in less than 100 years. Long-term comets may take as long as 30 million years to complete one trip around the Sun.

❯ Halley's Comet, which passes near Earth about every 76 years, could be seen from Easter Island in the South Pacific Ocean in 1986.

Digging Deeper

Your Challenge!

Voyager 1 began its journey through the solar system in 1977. It will continue traveling into interstellar space, the space between the stars. To dig deeper into the issue:

NASA has set up a website with information about *Voyager 1* and 2. Using this website and other sources, make a timeline of *Voyager 1*'s journey. Check back from time to time, and keep your timeline up-to-date.

Summary

The Kuiper belt, beyond Neptune, is home to thousands of objects, including four dwarf planets.

Further Inquiry

Earth's Moon is our planet's nearest neighbor. Maybe we should ask:

What is the Moon like?

What Is the Moon Like?

About 239,000 miles (385,000 km) from Earth, the Moon is 2,160 miles (3,475 km) wide. It appears bright because it reflects light from the Sun. The Moon makes one orbit of Earth in a little more than 27 days. It takes the same amount of time to rotate once on its axis. Because the two times are alike, the same side of the Moon is always facing Earth.

The Moon is made of rock very much like the types of rock found on Earth. The surface of the Moon visible from Earth has dark-colored and light-colored areas. The dark regions are covered with a rock called basalt, which formed when huge pools of lava cooled. The other regions have many different types of light-colored rock.

Much of the Moon is covered with soil. Moon soil can be anywhere from 3 to 65 feet (1 to 20 m) deep. On Earth, soil forms as wind and water wear away rock. On the Moon, where there is no atmosphere to burn up meteoroids, meteorites crashing into the surface and shattering rock created the soil. Large meteorites have blasted out craters in the Moon's surface.

Before people explored the Moon, scientists had three theories about its origin. One theory was that it used to be part of Earth. Another was that it formed near Earth. The third was that it formed somewhere in space and was captured by Earth's gravity. A recent new theory states that the Moon was formed when a giant asteroid struck Earth. The impact sent material from Earth into space. This material came together to form the Moon.

⌄ The first U.S. astronauts to walk on the Moon left an American flag on its surface.

Digging Deeper

Your Challenge!

The Apollo Program was developed by NASA to land humans on the Moon and return them safely to Earth. To dig deeper into the issue:

Research the *Apollo 11* mission that landed the first people on the Moon in 1969, as well as earlier missions leading up to it. List several major challenges NASA scientists and astronauts had to overcome to make *Apollo 11* a success. Explain how each of these challenges was met.

Summary

The Moon is made of rock very similar to Earth's. It is covered with craters caused by meteorites.

Further Inquiry

The Moon is not the only object in the night sky. Maybe we should ask:

What are stars and galaxies?

What Are Stars and Galaxies?

The universe includes many billions of stars. From Earth, only a few thousand stars can be seen with the human eye. The others are too far away to be visible to people looking up at the night sky.

The distance to stars is often measured in light-years. A light-year is the distance light travels in one year. The speed of light is 186,282 miles (299,792 km) per second. Therefore, one light-year is almost 6 trillion miles (10 trillion km). When people view a star, they are really seeing the way it looked in the past, at the time the light started its journey to Earth. For distant stars, this may be hundreds or even thousands of years back in time.

> Regulus is one of the brightest stars in the night sky. Its name comes from the Latin word for "king."

A galaxy is a collection of billions of stars. The Sun is in a galaxy called the Milky Way. It is only one of billions of galaxies in the universe. The Milky Way is a spiral galaxy, shaped like water going down a drain. Spiral galaxies are the most common, but some galaxies have oval, circular, or other shapes.

Galaxies form groups called clusters. The Milky Way belongs to a cluster of about 30 galaxies called the Local Group. The Milky Way is the second-largest galaxy in the Local Group. The largest is the Andromeda Galaxy. It contains 300 billion stars.

▼ Scientists have given one spiral galaxy the nickname Silver Dollar Galaxy because of its color and shape.

Digging Deeper

Your Challenge!

People in ancient cultures looked at the night sky and saw patterns that they thought looked like people or animals. These patterns are called constellations. To dig deeper into the issue:

Research constellations that are visible where you live. There are "star-finder" apps, or programs, available for many types of computers. On a night when it is not cloudy, go outside with an adult and try to locate constellations in the night sky.

Summary

The distance to a star is often measured in light-years. Stars are arranged in galaxies, and galaxies form clusters. The Milky Way is part of a cluster called the Local Group.

Further Inquiry

Stars do not go on shining forever. Maybe we should ask:

What are black holes and supernovas?

What Are Black Holes and Supernovas?

Stars can remain very hot for billions of years. Their "fuel" is the hydrogen deep inside that changes to helium, releasing heat. When a star runs out of fuel, it cools off. As it cools, the star collapses. Gases from the outer areas of the star move toward the center. The star gets smaller and smaller. Its density increases as **molecules** of gas are squeezed into less and less space. The dying star's gravity becomes stronger because the star is so dense. When a large star collapses, it sometimes turns into a black hole. A black hole has such strong gravity that nothing, not even light, can break free from it.

▼ When a star explodes, particles are blasted into space at a speed of 9,000 to 25,000 miles (15,000 to 40,000 km) per second.

▲ Before a star dies, helium that builds up inside it may start to burn. When this happens, scientists call the star a red giant.

Scientists cannot see black holes because no light escapes. Astronomers locate a black hole by observing the effects of its strong gravity. This gravity pulls other objects in space toward the black hole. In addition, when light from other stars passes near a black hole, its gravity bends the rays of light.

Supernovas are exploding stars. Often, the explosion occurs when a very large star is dying. While the star burned for billions of years, other substances were changed into iron deep inside the star. When the star burns out and molecules collapse toward the center, the iron becomes hotter and hotter. It may become so hot that the star explodes. A supernova explosion is very powerful. It may be millions of times brighter than the Sun. The amount of energy released by the explosion may be more than the energy sent out by the Sun in 10 billion years.

Digging Deeper

Your Challenge!

Supernovas that scientists can observe do not occur often. To dig deeper into the issue:

Research the supernova that took place in 1987. In what galaxy did it occur? What information did scientists gather about the size of this explosion? When was the last known supernova before the 1987 explosion?

Summary

Stars often shine for billions of years. As large stars burn out, some turn into black holes. Others may explode.

Further Inquiry

Where there are stars, it is possible that planets are orbiting them. Maybe we should ask:

Is there life on other planets?

Is There Life On Other Planets?

Three things are necessary for life. One is water. Another is organic compounds, which are chemicals that contain carbon. A third is a source of energy, such as the Sun.

Scientists believe a water ocean may exist below the frozen surface of Jupiter's moon Europa. Photographs taken by the spacecraft *Galileo* and by the Hubble Space Telescope seemed to show water coming up to the surface. The *Cassini* spacecraft found evidence of an ocean below the icy surface of Saturn's moon Enceladus. Scientists are studying both moons as places to look for signs of life.

Some scientists believe that, in the past, Mars may have had all the things needed for life. Water may exist deep inside the planet. At one time, there may have been water at the planet's surface. A meteorite from Mars contained traces of substances that could have come from ancient living things.

Scientists study exoplanets for signs of life. It is difficult to gather information about these bodies because they are so far away. One way that scientists search for life is by listening. Radio signals from Earth are constantly going into space. Some people wonder if forms of life on other planets may also be producing such signals. Using devices called radio telescopes, scientists hope they might hear a signal from some other solar system.

⌄ Radio telescopes can be aimed to listen for signs of life on planets identified by scientists as being "Earth-like."

Digging Deeper

Your Challenge!

The SETI Institute is one organization researching life on other planets. SETI stands for Search for Extraterrestrial Intelligence. To dig deeper into the issue:

Select the SETI Institute or another group doing similar research. Read about the organization's efforts to find life. What type of technology is the group using? Why did it choose this technology? What information has been gathered so far?

Summary

Scientists believe there once may have been life on Mars.

Further Inquiry

Using probes, space telescopes, and other technology, scientists have already learned a great deal about the universe in recent years. Taking all we have learned, maybe we finally can answer:

What is space?

Putting It All Together

Space has vast areas of emptiness, but it also contains a variety of objects. In Earth's solar system, there are planets orbiting the Sun and moons orbiting most of the planets. In the asteroid belt and the Kuiper belt, there are rocky or icy objects ranging in size from a grain of sand to dwarf planets nearly as large as the Moon. The Sun is one of billions of stars in the Milky Way galaxy. Beyond the Milky Way, there are billions of other galaxies in the universe. Astronomers continue to study the solar system and other stars in space. They search for answers to questions such as, Are there other solar systems like ours? Is there life on other planets?

❯ Each launch of a spacecraft marks the beginning of a new exploration into space. Some probes will travel for years before reaching their destination.

Where People Fit In

The study of space is one of the fastest-changing areas of science. Just 60 years ago, no satellites or probes had been sent into space. No humans had traveled in space. Today, hundreds of spacecraft have explored and continue to explore the solar system and beyond. People have walked on the Moon. Scientists and other astronauts spend months conducting research at the International Space Station that orbits Earth. Private companies have started to sell tickets for future space travel. Advances in technology and the process of scientific inquiry have allowed scientists to greatly increase their understanding of space and all it contains. This new information is shared with and has fascinated billions of people around the world.

Space Careers

Astronaut

The word *astronaut* comes from two Greek words that mean "space sailor." Astronauts need certain skills and experience before they can travel in space. Astronauts have a college degree and have studied mathematics, science, and engineering. Many astronauts are pilots. NASA astronauts who command missions must have at least 1,000 hours of experience flying jets. Often, they have gained flying experience in the military. An astronaut must be in good health, be fit, and have sharp vision. Space travel puts stress on the body, and astronauts must also be prepared to deal with any problems that may occur during a flight.

Astronomer

Astronomers work in many settings as they study outer space and the objects found there. Some astronomers work at government agencies, such as NASA. Some are employed at research organizations and museums. Many astronomers work at colleges and universities, where they conduct research and teach students. Most astronomers have spent many years in school studying mathematics and science, especially physics. They have at least a college degree. Many astronomers have advanced degrees. Computers skills are very important. An astronomer often works as part of a research team. He or she needs to be able to work well as a team member. In addition, it is important for an astronomer to be able to write well, so that he or she can explain discoveries to others.

Young Scientists at Work

The Moon appears to change shape at different times of the month. At first, it looks like a complete circle of light in the sky. This is called a full Moon. Over the following days, it slowly changes to a half-circle and to a quarter-circle. Then, it appears to have become completely dark, which is called a new Moon. After that, the bright area becomes larger again. The Moon's different shapes are called phases. You can demonstrate the cause of the phases of the Moon.

Materials
Pencil
Styrofoam ball at least 2 inches (5 cm) wide
Table lamp with the shade removed
Room that can be completely darkened

Instructions
1. Poke the pencil into the Styrofoam ball.

2. Place the lamp on a table or stool and turn it on. Except for the lamp, turn off all lights in the room and keep out sunlight.

3. Hold the ball in front of you like a lollipop and face the lamp so you can see both the ball and the lamp. The lamp is the Sun, and the ball is the Moon.

4. Keep your arm out straight in front of you and watch what happens to the light on the ball as you turn slowly to the left.

5. Stop when you have turned one-fourth of the way around. Stop again at halfway, and again at three-fourths of the way around.

Observations
Think about how what you saw as you turned compares to the phases of the Moon.

At which point or points did you see a new Moon, a half Moon, and a full Moon?

How do the positions of the Sun and Moon determine which phase of the Moon is visible from Earth?

Some scientists and other people have begun planning a space colony on Mars, where humans would live and work. If such a colony existed, would you want to be a space colonist? What would life be like for a person living on Mars?

Mars colonists need to have ways to get food, air, water, and heat. What technology could be used to grow food on Mars? How could people get air to breathe and water to drink? Where would power come from to heat buildings and run machinery?

How far is Mars from Earth? How long would it take a spacecraft carrying people to get there? How could colonists return to Earth if they wanted to or needed to?

What types of skills would it be important for Mars colonists to have? For example, how would they deal with sickness or injuries? How would they repair any equipment that broke?

What could colonists do with their waste? How could materials be reused and recycled?

Key Words

astronomers: scientists who study the universe and objects in space

atmosphere: the layer of gases surrounding a planet

axis: an imaginary line that runs through the center of a planet or other object in space

craters: bowl-shaped areas in which the ground is much lower than in the surrounding region

friction: a force that causes an object to slow down as a result of rubbing against something

glaciers: large areas of slow-moving ice, often found in cold mountainous regions

gravity: a force of attraction that draws two objects together

microorganisms: tiny forms of life that can be seen by humans only with the aid of a microscope

molecules: the smallest particles of a substance, composed of one or more atoms

oval: a shape that is similar to a circle but that is longer than it is wide

particles: very small pieces of something

planet: an object in space that travels around a star, such as Earth circling the Sun

probe: a spacecraft that has no crew

radar: a system that detects and provides information about objects by bouncing radio waves off them

radiation: energy in the form of waves or particles

satellite: a natural or human-made object that orbits a planet, moon, or other object in space

universe: all of space, including the stars, planets, and other objects

Index

Log on to www.av2books.com

AV² by Weigl brings you media enhanced books that support active learning. Go to www.av2books.com, and enter the special code found on page 2 of this book. You will gain access to enriched and enhanced content that supplements and complements this book. Content includes video, audio, weblinks, quizzes, a slide show, and activities.

AV² Online Navigation

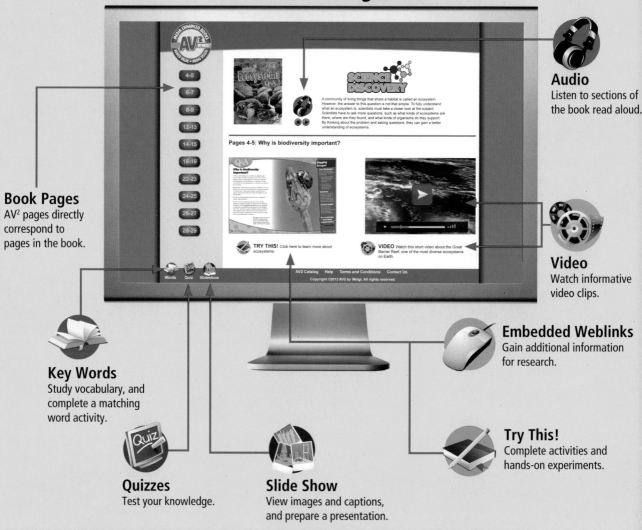

Book Pages
AV² pages directly correspond to pages in the book.

Audio
Listen to sections of the book read aloud.

Video
Watch informative video clips.

Embedded Weblinks
Gain additional information for research.

Key Words
Study vocabulary, and complete a matching word activity.

Try This!
Complete activities and hands-on experiments.

Quizzes
Test your knowledge.

Slide Show
View images and captions, and prepare a presentation.

AV² was built to bridge the gap between print and digital. We encourage you to tell us what you like and what you want to see in the future.

Sign up to be an AV² Ambassador at www.av2books.com/ambassador.